soul's
epiphany

Table of Contents

Table of Contents

Section II: Self-Love

Table of Contents

soulxsigh

Prologue

A room full of voices,
mine felt lost.
Back to my own world,
I began to write.

I thought to myself,

*What is the point of their belief
in the unrealistic
when they stopped believing
their dreams long ago?*

Love

Do you remember the constellations
we named together under the night sky?
How each star that night felt like our own secret.
I remember how we lay there, side by side,
the world quiet around us,
and it was just us and the rest of the world.

I can still feel the cool grass beneath us,
and the crisp wind that hinted us closer.
We traced the sky with our fingertips
and named constellations after our favorite memories.
Midnight Looks was one of them.

Those moments felt endless,
as if the entire universe was holding its breath
just for us.
We were more than just two people then.
We were explorers and dreamers.

No matter where life takes us,
those stars will always be ours.
And even now, when the world feels heavy,
I look up at our stars,
because no matter what,
those constellations will always remind me of you.

And I hope that when you look up,
you see our stars, too.

Falling for you wasn't just falling.
Falling for you was like standing still,
feeling the ground beneath my feet,
and knowing where I was and exactly where I wanted to
be.

Falling for you was a light that kissed my soul
and made me believe in the beauty of beginnings.

Now I know that not every love
has a dramatic rise and fall.
Some connections just have a steady presence of love,
a love that feels right and true,
with no need for anything more.

Peace. That's what you gave me.
Warm nights,
relaxed shoulders,
and drooping eyelids.
You showed me what it meant to be cared for.

Contentment. That's what I gave you.
Presence in stillness,
reassurance,
and unconditional love.
A balanced mind and a place turned into something
called home.

Epiphany. That's what we gave each other.
Focused hearts,
clarity,
and rose-colored vision;
secret looks,
and a love-filled mission.
I can't help but tell you,
it's your heart I want to visit.

Existence. That's what changed when our souls collided.
Suddenly heard heartbeats growing closer,
blending forever but never imagined.
I would change the world for you,
if only you and I were always together.

Lifetimes of you.
Lifetimes for you.
Endless nights endured in patient sorrow,
waiting to find the one who makes the wait worthwhile.
To discover you, to know you, is to find a million reasons
to never relinquish the dream of us.
For a thousand lifetimes, I would wait
just to spend one moment with you.
Lifetimes have led me to you,
and I will spend lifetimes loving you.
For knowing you are my end, I would brave it all.

If you asked me if I love you, I'd say yes. But if you asked me again...

I'd say my love for you is immutable. It's in the way I can't stop thinking about you even when I'm busy, or how you listen to me ramble about nothing and everything. It's how everything is better when you're a part of it, and how I feel complete when I'm with you and lost when I'm not. I would tell you that I love you like deep conversations love rooftop views, or like how I love the moments we steal away from the world and make our own. And I would tell you how even a look from you sends shivers down my spine, or how I love that your voice softens when you say my name. To love you is to love the layers of your history that have shaped you, and every new layer that comes. It's to taste new beginnings and to dream of a thousand tomorrows.

It began with a glance.
A moment noticed by the world
but never forgotten by us.

I left after meeting you,
not realizing how much you would mean to me.
You were the start of something special
that I never saw coming.

You know what ***the truest love is?*** The love that comes with no signs. The kind of love that pops up into your life when you aren't looking for it. The kind that comes out of nowhere, and you feel your entire world turn. True love comes completely without warning, without any chance to think about it or process it. Almost like how a storm rolls in from a clear sky, the sudden downpour drowning you in emotions you didn't know existed. It's the love that bursts in, like a flower growing through concrete, because love doesn't care who you are or what's around it. It's fierce and fervent, and it shatters the walls you built around yourself. And then you realize that everything you thought about love was wrong. You realize that love is as simple as the undeniable emotional pull that draws you to one another endlessly. It's the unmistakable signal in a world of static.

Her eyes,
they see every true thing deep within me.
Her lips,
they paint words in the air like delicate butterflies.
Her gaze,
deeper than oceans, vaster than the skies.
Her energy,
a pulsating force, vivacious and bright.
Her silhouette,
a gentle outline against the evening sky.
Her aroma,
a blend of blooming flowers and a lightning-struck night.
Every single part of her,
perfections that nobody can change.

soulxsigh

My soul does sigh for you.
Big gasps for breath
I took after realizing I was holding it
while looking at your face.

You could simply walk
or even run, jump, fall in the mud,
or tear your dress on a branch,
I would still think you move with grace.

And when they asked me how I
can love someone like that,
I only thought of one name.

I sigh

Because your soul lights mine on fire,
but that's not something that you should take blame.

11

In the most selfish way possible,
I want to be the only one who has your heart,
I want to be the one who understands it completely.
The one who holds it close.

I don't want anyone else to feel your touch,
or the warmth of you just being close.

I don't want anyone else to kiss your lips,
to taste the sweetness that I love.
I want to be the one who kisses you goodnight,
and wakes up to you each morning.

I want to be the reason you smile,
to catch the light in your eyes
from the smallest things that make you happy.
I want to be the one who brings you happiness,
who makes you laugh until you cry.

I want us to be in the same book,
and to end in the same chapter.

I want to be your last everything.
In the most selfish way possible,
I want all of you forever.

We cannot always flee the shadows.
Our love was tested and proven through sorrows.
Our path was beautiful because of the courage we found
to walk on it.
Our love was forged in fire,
and that's what makes it unbreakable.
Together we face it all.

soul's epiphany

How could *a love like this* be anything but destined?
We are not merely two souls passing in the night.

Our love was carefully sculpted by the hands of fate; it
has always been meant to be.

When you are absent, the sun loses its brilliance,
as if the cosmos itself acknowledges my sorrow.
This is not just a need dictated by loneliness
or the void that accompanies human existence.

This is the connection that fills an emptiness
that would never be complete without you.

Love is effort.
Love is understanding.
Love is forgiving.
Love is trusting.
Love is listening.
Love is empathy.
Love is vulnerability.
Love is selflessness.
Love is timeless.
Love is sacrifice.
Love is passion.
Love is unconditional.
Love is an unspoken promise.
Love is home.

There's not a single day that passes
that I don't go to sleep
without thinking about how
you touched my soul...

soulxsigh

Your memory lingers like a sweet scent in the air,
always stuck in my mind, it never fades.
I guess that's how a memory works,
binding itself to your consciousness
to remind you of the moments
that have long passed yet are vividly alive.

But maybe that's a good thing because, truthfully,
I would never want to forget about you.
How did you become a part of me
when you're not even here?

Here I stand in emptiness
where your voice might fill the air once more.
I find the agony of your absence
fighting with the lingering touch of your love.

You are my bittersweet memory,
constantly tugging on the strings of my soul.
You shape my thoughts,
you guide my dreams,
and you help me feel every emotion.
Even in the end, your memory
will stay with me.

You are most beautiful when you're not looking.
When you're lost in your thoughts, just being yourself,
you radiate an elegance that is indescribable.
The way you sit in your own natural grace is completely
captivating.
Your beauty then is real and unfiltered.
Who knew daydreaming could look so beautiful?
No memory, photograph, or painting
could ever capture the essence of you.
They can't hold the raw honesty of your soul.
They can't reflect the electric presence you have the
moment you arrive.
These moments of you are quite breathtaking in their
simplicity.
You, simply being yourself, is the most beautiful vision
I've ever known.

I want all of you. Every struggle, every tear, every fear. You deserve to be loved deeply, fully, without hesitation. I want to be your rock, your safe place, your never-ending reminder that you matter to someone deeply. Your pain is mine, your joy is mine. You deserve someone who loves you for who you are and who cherishes your soul.

Your heart is a beautiful masterpiece that I lose track of reality adoring.

You said you wonder who will really be there for you, and I'm here to tell you that I'm that person. I am here, ready to love you, ready to be there for you, always.

One more day with you would mean the world.
To bridge the gap between us that time created.
A day to reminisce on all we've missed.
We could walk through all the memories we once shared.
One more day to delve into everything
unspoken between us.
One more day to understand each other better.
It would be one more chance to show you my
appreciation for you,
to celebrate your presence in my life
and how much you matter to me.
Just one more day could make a difference.
One more day to trace the contours of your soul
with the fingertips of mine,
to explore the depth of what we were
and what we could be together.
One more day to stare into your eyes,
where the sun finds envy in the light
that shines from them,
to see the reflection of my own feelings mirrored back.
One more day to listen to the silence between us,
and the peace that comes from that.

The saddest thing I've ever heard
was when you stepped onto the bus,
and you turned back to me and said:

"Maybe we'll get to see each other again
in another life."

Do you miss me?
Do you miss me like I missed you
when you left me wondering if we would be together
forever like you said we would?

Do you miss me like when I missed you
when I had to be gone for six months,
and I couldn't speak to you,
or hear you, or feel you, or touch you?

Do you miss me like when I miss you
every night I sleep alone in my bed,
really struck with insomnia
because my mind is always busy missing you?

Do you miss me like when I miss you
even every second we are together
because being with you makes me terrified of the next
moment we won't be in each other's arms?

Do you miss me like I miss how we used to talk for hours
and never run out of things to say?
Do you miss me like I miss the comfort,
the certainty from just knowing you were there?

Because, for me, I miss you in all of those ways.
You're right in front of me, all mine,
and I still miss you.
I will never not miss you.

22

Can love last forever? I believe it can.
Real love is not just a feeling. It is a commitment, a decision to care, to support, and to stand by someone through the ups and downs. It is being there in the worst times and the best times.

Love is understanding and forgiving.

It does not diminish with time. Instead, it grows, it deepens, and it evolves. It endures through changes, and it is a bond that strengthens with every experience. Love is a constant effort to show kindness, to offer support, and to be present in every moment. It is a choice to prioritize someone, to value their happiness as much as your own.

True love is selfless.

It is patient, and it does not waver even when circumstances change.

Love, in its truest form, is everlasting.

A soulmate won't arrive knowing all your secrets.
They won't understand your past with perfect clarity.
They'll learn you in small fragments,
what makes you shine and what makes you tick.
They won't have a specific guide to your heart,
and charting the map of your soul comes with no ease.
But they will listen,
and they will stay through the
loudest and most silent moments in your life.

True soulmates don't appear fully formed,
but they grow alongside you,
and that's how they come *to know your soul.*

When you fall in love with someone
that you never expected to fall for...
that is the most beautiful kind of love.

It catches you off guard,
turns your world upside down,
yet feels right anyway.
There is no expectation,
just raw, unfiltered emotion.

It's almost like it starts off as a secret,
quietly and unknown.
But then suddenly, it's only this love that fills your mind.
And every new thing you learn about them
is an unexpected thrill.

You'll notice a subtle shift in different parts of your life,
like how your thoughts naturally and constantly
drift towards them,
or how you feel more fulfilled at the most boring times
and the most exciting times with them.

And then you'll finally realize that true love
doesn't have to be planned, expected, or sought after,
because love finds you when you least expect it,
and there's no other love like that.

You are the dream
of a future
I never want to wake from.

Every second
is worth more
than a lifetime
without you.

soulxsigh

I was not expecting you,
nor was my soul searching for anyone.
Yet you showed up
as if the moon had whispered my need.

To peer into your eyes
was to see if the feeling coursing through my bones
was the same coming from your words.
To know whether my heart could entrust itself to you.
Because a shattered heart
was something I couldn't sweep off the floor this time.

But I knew that those eyes were a dangerous game
because as soon as I looked,
every defense I once had dissolved completely.
That's when I knew I didn't have to clench my heart
so tightly anymore.

Thank you for finding me.
I promise this to you my love,
within my arms you shall find your home.

Until we see each other again,
know that you dwell in my heart.
That's where I will keep you
until the day we never have to part.

Maybe love is meant to drive us mad. Because love is like water slipping through our fingers.

It's a paradox, really.

We crave the permanence of love, but we never realize how fast it can evaporate the moment we look away. Love is an intangible feeling, and maybe that's why it almost feels like a figment of our imagination. How is it that something so powerful, so capable of shaping our lives, remains beyond our complete understanding? Love is a reminder that prioritizing what truly matters is a necessity. The chaos that love brings is both bewildering and beautiful. It makes everything that we find certain shaken up. We question our beliefs, we grapple with doubts, we relive our fears, and we indulge in the intensity of our feelings. Love is a winding path with a thousand mirrors that leads us to a place that only the future knows of. It pushes us to lose and refind ourselves over and over until we are at the brink of what we truly desire out of love.

But only the ones brave enough to go through this are the ones who find that everlasting connection.

Every breath I take is yours,
and you couldn't give me a clue
on how I could love you more.

Every breath you take is mine,
and I wouldn't see anything else
but your light,

Even in the silence
left by long goodbyes.

I got addicted to you so easily.
Attracted to you in ways that are hard to explain.
Every day, you're in my head.
When night falls, and the world quiets,
my mind doesn't.
It's filled with thoughts of you.

I lay awake, wanting to talk to you.
You're the last whisper in my consciousness
before sleep claims me,
and my first thought when I wake.
This is how every day goes.

I care about you more than you realize,
and I appreciate you more than you think.
Please tell me every time our eyes meet,
you feel what I feel
and tell me that I'm not the only one
wide awake right now,
stuck in a trance of wishing you were here.

Tell me that I'm not the only one
picking up my phone every minute
of every night instead of sleeping,
just waiting for you to let me hear your voice
and all of your sweet thoughts.

I want only your attention.
And with that,
I'll find my peace.

You took my soul
ripped it out of my chest
I fell to the deepest point
one could fall

but then you returned it
parts of you added

Now I can't imagine
being who I was
without you.

I think I love you too much.
It's a weight, a darkness that pulls
at the core of my being.
Like a shadow, it's inseparable from me,
moving as I move, breathing as I breathe.

In this love, I find a quiet despair,
an echo of something profound yet unsettling.
It's not the love that poets glorify, or songs celebrate.
It's a love that consumes, burns, and leaves nothing but
ashes of what once was.

I fear this love,
for it is not just an emotion,
but a relentless force that reshapes my very existence.
To love you too much is to lose myself in the abyss of
you, to dissolve into the darkness
that your absence creates.

There is no solace in this love,
only an unending thirst that no affection can quench.
Each day, I wrestle with the paradox
of wanting you closer yet fearing
the engulfing tide of my own emotions.

To love you too much is a curse,
a beautiful, tragic curse that I bear silently.
For in this love, I am both the prisoner and the jailer,
locked away by my own heart's unyielding grip.

Is there a mystery deeper than the alchemy of two hearts
beating as one?
A fusion of souls so intense that it overshadows
all the wonders of the world.
How is it that love can bend your reality,
and can make you wake up in another world just by
looking into the eyes of someone you love?
It can be so blinding that it changes you before
you can realize something's different.
If I had to choose one word to define love,
I would say selflessness.
Is love not the root that keeps us grounded while
the winds of life try to sway us?
Do we not all search the heavens for a sign
that love is our true north?
Love isn't easy to define,
yet no one can deny its impact.
And though love can end in heartbreak, even then,
it leaves us with lessons about who we are and what we
want from life.
Love is a fundamental part of being human.

The deepest connections require no words.
This is the **paradox of love:**
to be profoundly known without a word,
to feel the resonance of another soul within your own
heart.

If two souls can bask in silence
without longing for words,
then their hearts have whispered secrets
to each other that language cannot capture.
Every sigh and every touch becomes a declaration.
Eyes meet, and in that glance,
volumes are spoken.
Hands touch, and in their warmth,
a dialogue richer than any penned letter unfolds.

If we were in the endless library of emotion,
our love would be the most articulate volume,
yet it wasn't written, it was lived.

And even when you and your beloved are far apart,
your shared memories draw you closer than ever.
Emotions in love are like the palette of the dusk sky:

ephemeral,
ever-shifting,
endlessly filled

with hues of passion and tenderness.

I didn't love you because I was lonely.
Far from it.
I was at peace in my own world,
wrapped in the comfort of solitude.

But then you appeared,
like a comet streaking across my night sky.
Your presence was more than just a spark.
It was a blaze that lit up my entire existence.

You made me open my eyes again,
to see the world in vivid color,
to feel life pulsing around me.
With you, every day is a revelation,
a journey into a world I never knew existed.

Losing you would be unimaginable,
like being plunged back into darkness.
It would leave a void so profound,
I doubt I could ever find my way back.

Nothing else matters as long as I'm with you.
As long as I have you, everything else pales in
comparison.
You are my everything, my absolute.

It really *made my soul sigh*
when you told me you loved me.
No, really.
Your words were simple,
yet they carried the weight of the world.

It was an understanding
that we are two separate souls,
yet somehow, we fit together.

Your words were like gentle rain
that gave me a breath of fresh air.

You're far away
but I want your presence closer to me.
My heart aches
even though I know you're thinking of me.
Distance separates us,
whether for a minute or a month;
it can't diminish my feelings.
You deserve all my love
even when we're apart.
Come closer,
because you mean everything to me.

I would never
become a ghost
to you.

If I lost you
I would turn
into one
and if you
left

The ghost
of your
presence
would haunt me
for the rest
of my
life.

They asked: What makes your heart race?
But I realized my heart hasn't stopped racing since I met you.

Then they asked what the most beautiful thing I'd ever seen was.
I said it was the sunlight glistening on your skin, making you look like a vision of pure beauty.

They asked where I find my peace.
I told them that the only time I feel peace is when you enter my presence and make everything else fade away.

They asked: What do you dream about the most?
I said it's a future where we wake up together every day.

They asked: What is your favorite word?
I said "home", because it's where you are.

And then they asked about my favorite feeling.
I instantly thought about the contentment of your hand in mine.

If everything happens for a reason,
can you be the reason that we begin?
Can we be the reason our hearts race
and we forget how we ended up here,
but we both know it was meant to be?
And now we know the reason was love.

Love me in the morning,
love me in the night,
love me with all of you,
love me before I die.

When the world feels cold,
and the shadows grow long,
love me with your warmth,
make me feel I belong.

From the moment *I first saw you*,
I promised myself
that my heart would never wander,
never seek another.
I vowed to love no one new,
to never feel for anyone
the way I feel for you.

My priority,
my deepest commitment,
is to make us last,
not just for a lifetime,
but far beyond that.

If I could tell you
all the reasons
why
I would never leave you
days would pass
and when we
finished talking
we would
realize
only a few
minutes
were lost.

Soulmates do exist. It took me a while to believe that, but now I know it's true. The reality is, you don't get to choose who you fall in love with, and you don't get to choose who falls in love with you. It's this uncontrollable force that just happens, and when it does, it changes everything.

You know they're your person when you can be tired together or bored together, but every moment is still full of the energy that's good for your soul. It's in those quiet moments, when nothing much is happening, that you realize how deeply connected you are. You look at each other and there's a comfort, a peace, that you can't find anywhere else.

And when you never want them to stop talking because hearing them makes the world not so quiet anymore, that's when you know. They take care of your heart and everything about you that no one else would care to know. They see the parts of you that you try to hide, and they love you even more for them.

There's not a single love that is perfect, but there are hundreds that are real. It's messy and beautiful and worth every single second. This is what love is. This is what it means to find your soulmate.

What if we never met?
My soul would wander aimlessly,
through life, longing for a love it never knew.

I walk through mist and moonlight,
searching for a reality that eludes me,
a world where your touch
never graced my soul.

What if we never breathed the same breath?
I don't think I'd be able to recognize
the sweet fragrance that defines you.

I'd forever be a sigh in the night,
a wisp in the wind,
a lost poet without words,
a broken light that can't fully shine,
a star that never found its constellation.

What if we never met?
I don't want to go back to those nights alone
that left my heart restless.
The nights when the stars were less bright,
and the moon was just a sliver of hope.

The very thought of life before you,
leaves me hollow
and fills me with chills all at once.

soulxsigh

Self Love

You can't fully give your heart to someone if you never gave it to yourself first. It's in ***nurturing your own soul*** that you find the strength to connect deeply with someone else.

The biggest lesson I've learned in life is that ***healing isn't about*** trying to make everything work perfectly all the time. It's about recognizing when you're pushing yourself too hard or understanding your limits and respecting them. I think most people think of healing as a destination or an end goal they want to get to, but most of the time, healing only works when you treat it like an ongoing process. You don't have to be everything to be worthy of love and happiness.

When you want to heal, what you really want is to bring a balance into your life between pursuing what makes you comfortable while also acknowledging the insecurities and fears you may have. When you do something or when you feel something, when you go through something, do you criticize yourself, or do you show yourself compassion and constructively fix the problem? One of the biggest learning curves is giving yourself the grace to make mistakes along the way. I used to think setbacks meant failure, but now I realize that it's all a part of the same journey. Sometimes, we forget that all we are is human and that we have to create a space within ourselves that makes us feel safe in our thoughts and emotions.

They always say **"*cheer up*"** when you're down,
but here's what I say to you:
There will be a day when the weight on your shoulders
feels lighter.
It's okay to not be okay all the time.
You don't have to force a smile
or pretend everything is fine when it's not.
Feeling down is part of being human.
It's a sign that you've been strong for too long,
that you need to take time to understand yourself,
to listen to what your heart needs.
Healing takes time,
and it's alright to give yourself that.
It's the dark moments that make the bright ones shine
even brighter.
You are allowed to feel, to be vulnerable.
And in this vulnerability, you will find your strength.
So don't rush yourself,
don't apologize for the changes in you.
There will be a day when you'll look back
and see how far you've come. And that day,
you'll realize your strength was with you all along.

You grow through what you go through. You never leave a challenge behind without learning something new. Life doesn't promise smooth journeys, but it guarantees growth for those who dare to tread its paths. Facing your fears teaches you courage. Making decisions teaches you responsibility.

Pain, as much as we despise it, is a profound teacher. It carves into us the capacity for empathy, deepens our understanding, and sculpts our spirit with endurance. Joy, on the other hand, teaches us gratitude, imbuing our days with light and our hearts with warmth. Both joy and pain are essential to getting anything out of life.

To grow through what you go through is to embrace life's duality, to understand that every moment, no matter how trivial or monumental, carries with it the seeds of wisdom.

This is the essence of being human: to learn, to adapt, and to evolve, transforming every experience into a stepping stone towards what you are seeking. The more you go through, the more you grow.

It's a lifelong process.

If life could speak to you,
It would say:

"I know you want comfort now,
but know you'll be happy in the future.
I must test you and push you
not to your limits but past them.
I must make you question everything
time and time again
until you find the strength
to allow your true happiness to blossom
from where you've been hiding it away.
I must do this for you
so you know that you deserve what you will earn
and so you start believing in yourself now."

To be authentic means to be the most unapologetic version of your true self. You don't have to like everything that everyone else likes, you don't have to do everything that everyone else does, and you especially don't have to be accepted by everyone you come across. All you have to do to be authentically you is to accept the beautiful things you hold.

Actions speak louder than words,
and what we do shouts so loud,
it drowns out what we say,
casting either shadows
or light on the road we walk.

Things are different now.
Colors don't seem the same,
ice cream doesn't taste as sweet,
and the sun doesn't feel as warm.
Every day used to bring something new,
now it feels like repetition,
and the air feels heavier when I sigh.
The one thing in my life that has been constant is change.

Call it inevitable.

The thing is, change keeps leading me somewhere
unexpected.
I've started to see happiness differently.
It's not in the brightness or warmth anymore.
It's in the deeper, quieter places,
where I can actually hear myself think.

Change was necessary.

You were once convinced that you'd never see the light of day, yet here you are. It's almost remarkable how we can feel so insurmountable when all we have to do is look back and see how many obstacles we've conquered. All the moments that shattered you didn't fully break you, did they? Love life because it is the one thing that never stops teaching you, testing you, and bringing you closer to understanding yourself. When you see no light around, remember, there's more light within you to pull you out of those dark times.

The longer you live, the more you learn to love your own company. And when you learn to love yourself, you realize you want to share your company with someone else who loves you just as much. It's then that you realize you could never have loved that person without first learning to love yourself. You see your own flaws and learn to embrace them, so why wouldn't you love someone else's flaws too? After all that, you finally understand that you have someone to give your heart to because loving yourself is when your heart grows.

Static life. When you wake up each day feeling the same, going through the motions, watching time pass by— sometimes quicker, sometimes slower—when each day blends into the next, and nothing seems to change or move in any direction. You see others moving on, growing, and changing, and you wonder why you are where you are.

Maybe it's a pause, a moment to breathe and reflect on all the places you've been. Maybe it's a chance to stop and fully appreciate everything you've experienced, to remember all the beautiful and challenging moments that shaped your character. It could be a time to reconnect with yourself and consider how you've been moving and treating yourself. Sometimes, you need to stand still to understand how you need to grow. What's the point in rushing if you're unsure of the right direction?

Static life. Or momentary clarity?

You push people away because you're scared
of getting hurt.
Some call it a defense mechanism,
I say it's just trying not to drown
in the same river twice.
Your shield was only crafted
from the old scars you glued together.

You shove people out
to protect yourself from another disappointment,
not seeing you're also tossing out any chance at a good
day, a real laugh, a warm hug.
Even the most fortified castles have their gates,
and letting someone in doesn't mean the walls you've built
start to crumble.
Opening up can feel like a gamble,
but it's also the door to experiences
that can't be lived alone.

Letting someone in is an art of discerning who can walk
alongside you without casting shadows on your path.
Being alone, sure, it makes you smart,
teaches you how to fight your own battles.
But even fighters need a corner,
someone to say the right word when it counts.
Life's short, and most people are a bad bet,
but now and then, someone can make you think twice.

Lately, I've been trying to figure out **what happiness really is.** Is it just those moments of breaking a smile for a little while, or is it a deep feeling of being content with life? I've started to see that happiness doesn't reside in the biggest moments or the most praise. It's about the little things that happen every day that we don't always notice. Maybe I just need to see what's right in front of me. These ordinary moments almost seem trivial. Feeling the sun on my face, breathing the fresh air right after it rains, seeing the stars twinkle in the clear night sky. Quiet magic that often slips through the fingers of those chasing after grander visions. These are soft little nudges reminding you to pause and soak in the world's subtle wonders. If happiness is made of these moments, then it's something I can have every day.

When you were alone, and you actually felt alone, you didn't let it overcome your mind. You didn't let it consume your willingness to try again. You didn't give up, and you didn't lose hope. You may not be able to control everything that happens in life, but what you can do is throw away the stress of not being perfect. You were never supposed to be anything more than who you wanted to be.

soulxsigh

Everyone is different. It's not as cliché as you think.
Someone is filled with ambition,
and someone else is content with simplicity. Some may
like the thrill of adventure, while someone else hates it
and prefers routine calmness. Someone always chooses to
avoid confrontation or conflict, and other people decide
to roll with the punches. The point is, not being you is the
only thing holding you back.

Self Improvement

Don't quit.
You've come so far already.
Look back at the beginning,
see how much ground you've covered.
It wasn't easy, right? But you did it.
Every step you took brought you here.
Don't stop now.
Not when you've proven to yourself how strong you are.

Remember that growth happens one step at a time.
Your journey is not over.
It's just getting tougher because you're moving closer to
something great.
Quitting might feel like an option when it's hard, but flip
that feeling.
Every challenge is a chance to grow even stronger.
Don't give up on the progress you've made.
You're closer than you think to the breakthrough you're
waiting for.

Keep pushing.
The hardest climbs often lead to the best views.
Stay the course.
Your future self will thank you.
So, don't quit.
You're right on the edge of victory.
Now repeat after me:

I. Will. Not. Quit.

You will never taste victory *if you fear the start.*
Hesitation is the enemy of success, and inaction is the
grave of potential. The beginning is the gateway to
everything you can achieve.

You did it. ***I'm so proud of you.*** You've finally reached your big goal after late nights and tough challenges, and it's all your doing. It's time to celebrate your accomplishments and soak up the results of your determination. This win is the base for whatever comes next and proof that you should be proud of yourself.

I want to see you win.
I want to see you achieve everything you aim for.
I hope you conquer all the obstacles in your path,
and I hope you reach success.
I'm cheering you on at every small step forward you take,
I will always be in your corner.
You are built for significant achievements.
My desire is for you to thrive.

I know today was tough. I know you might not be where you want to be yet. I know it's harder to see the end goal when the entire path is still ahead of you. But let me tell you something very important. Your commitment to perseverance speaks volumes. Don't be too hard on yourself. You can't keep being the first person in line to dismiss your own hard work. It doesn't matter if someone is further along than you. It doesn't matter if someone started before you. It doesn't matter how much further you have to go. It's easy to forget that your small steps forward are still moving you forward, so trust in it, and allow it to spark something inside you. Any moment you face the choice to pursue or to sit back is the exact chance to turn your life around and become unstoppable. Believe in yourself. You can achieve great things.

Who are you beyond the surface?
You're not just a collection of moments and memories.
You are a story still being written.
Dig deep inside yourself;
you hold worlds of dreams,
oceans of fears,
and mountains of hope.
Your heart is a world rich with the complexities
of who you are and who you could be.
You embody so much more than you realize.

They say **_your twenties_** are the foundation of your future,
but it often feels like building on shifting sand.
I often wonder if the person I am becoming
is the one I wanted to be.
We find ourselves at the crossroads
of expectation and desire,
searching for a path that feels like our own.
We are constantly negotiating
between the person we are
and the person we wish to become.

I realize now that growth
is less about becoming someone new
and more about shedding who I'm not.
Personal growth often comes
from the most unexpected experiences.
The pressure to succeed
often outweighs the fear of failure.
Memories shape our perception of the present
and expectations for the future.

Not all friendships are meant to last,
and that's okay.
We often fear the unknown
until it becomes familiar.
I stand at the edge of tomorrow,
wondering which dreams will survive the dawn.

I laid my head down on my pillow and **woke up in my dreams.** And when I looked around, I saw thousands of me staring back at me. I realized that reality and dreams had merged into one. Each one was a reflection of a different choice, a path I could have taken, or a word I could have said. Time didn't exist here, and emotions flowed freely. I could see my joy, my sorrow, my courage, and my fears. They lived in worlds shaped by decisions I never made, loved in ways I never dared, and cried tears I never shed. I wandered through landscapes crafted from my deepest hopes. I was more than just myself. I woke up and realized I was half asleep in life. I was faced with the risks I should have taken, the mistakes that I never acknowledged, and the goals and dreams that I stuffed away. You have to live fully to realize that growth and comfort rarely coexist.

soulxsigh

You did good today. Really good.
You might not see it,
you might think it was just another day,
but it wasn't.
Every step you took today was a step forward,
no matter how small.

You faced challenges,
you overcame obstacles, and you kept moving.
Remember, every effort counts,
every bit of progress matters.
You're building a better tomorrow
with every action you take today.

The struggles you faced?
They're just stepping stones,
leading you to greater heights.
You're stronger than you realize,
more capable than you give yourself credit for.
Be proud of yourself.

You're doing the work, making things happen.
Your journey is unique,
and every twist and turn is shaping you
into the incredible person you are meant to be.
Sleep well, knowing that you are on the right path.

You may feel like you are in ***a dark room*** alone,
unable to find the light switch,
but remember, every room has a door,
a door that leads somewhere else, somewhere brighter.
You are not alone in this room.
Many have been here before, some are here now.
They, too, are searching for the light switch or the door.
You might not see them, but they are there.
The dark room is not the whole world;
it's just a small part of a much bigger place,
a place filled with light and color and life.
You will leave this room eventually.
It's not a matter of if, but when.
The strength to stand up, to search for the light switch or
the door,
is within you. It always has been.
Sometimes, it just takes a little longer to find it,
but you will, and when you step out of this room into the
light,
you'll see just how strong you really are.
Until then, remember you are not alone in the dark,
and the light is waiting for you just beyond the door.

There comes *a time in our lives when we realize* the journey to uncover who we are demands letting go of everything that does not propel us forward. It's a crucial turning point, where we must peel away the layers of expectations, fears, and past identities that have clung to us over the years. It's neither easy nor painless, but it is essential for growth. Our true path emerges not by seeking everything that is new but by looking at what we already have in front of us with a new perspective. This is the heart of finding our purpose, having the bravery to discard the unnecessary, to allow the core of our being to thrive. The heaviest load we bear often isn't our challenges but our reluctance to release them. If we can stop holding ourselves back from our true aspirations, dreams can become our reality because they lead our lives with authenticity and intention.

The mind is a strange place.
It holds universes within silent walls.
Thoughts run wild
and dreams build cities overnight.
Fears create monsters out of shadows
and hope lights up dark corners.

The mind is a battlefield.
Ideas clash and emotions wage war.
Memories hide in every crevice
and whisper stories of what was.
The future is inevitable
and some memories are forgotten.

The mind bends time.
Seconds either stretch into hours
or years go by in a blink.
It's constantly living in
yesterdays,
todays,
and tomorrows.

The mind is a sanctuary.
A place to hide when the world gets too loud.
A gallery of personal masterpieces
painted with thoughts no one else sees.

But it's also a prison.

Would you erase a painful memory if it meant losing the lessons it taught you?

Can we truly forgive if we can't forget what happened?

Can you truly appreciate joy without experiencing sorrow?

Does questioning ourselves help us grow or just hold us back?

Do we see the world as it is or as we are?

Is our identity defined more by our intentions or by our actions?

If you could see the future but change nothing, would you want to know?

Can what we dream about at night change how we act during the day?

If happiness could be purchased, would it hold the same value?

Would you choose a life of happiness without achievement or a life full of achievements but with no real happiness?

Is love the ultimate truth or the greatest illusion?

I was letting life eat me alive.
But one day, I woke up and realized something pivotal.
You'll be miserable with life until you dance in the rain.

Life grinds you down.
I stopped running, stood still,
let the rain hit me.
That was the moment I started to heal.

Don't wait for storms to pass,
embrace the water as it falls.
The sun does not always have to shine
for you to find your own light.

You don't have to be held down
by the weight of your worries.
We're all just walking through mud,
pretending it's a red carpet.

But there's something about puddles,
jumping in, not caring
it's the closest we get to freedom.

This is how I want to live:
facing the hard,
enjoying the good,
and embracing the change.

Don't give up just because no one is coming to save you.
Get up and show everyone why they should have.

We share the same sky,
yet see different horizons.
I wonder how the same heavens
that cradle my dreams
cast a different glow on your path.

We stare at the same stars,
yet the stories they tell us
are as varied as the souls that listen.
And while our views differ,
the sky doesn't care for our preferences.

soulxsigh

soul's epiphany

Epilogue

Words are like breaths
poems are heartbeats

Graced pages
touched my soul
clearer vision
it gave me

Dreams are alive,
hope is the pulse.

As the final word fades
and you learn serendipity is true
savor its immensity
let the soft glow
of a dream guide you.

To my incredible community,

As I look back on the journey that led me to create this book, I am filled with immense gratitude. This collection of poetry is not just a compilation of words; it is a symbol of the support, love, and encouragement that I have received from each one of you.

Nothing makes this more worthwhile than being a part of a community that uplifts and inspires each other to chase their dreams, believe in love, and make a difference in the world. This book would not have been possible without your support. Every comment, share, and message of encouragement has meant the world to me and fueled my passion to keep writing and sharing my words with you.

You have not only motivated me but have pushed me to explore deeper layers of my craft. Together, we have created a community that thrives on growth and love.

I thank each and every one of you from the bottom of my heart. Let's continue to dream, love, and explore the infinite possibilities. I can't wait to see what the future holds.

Love,

soulxsigh

Visions

soulxsigh

soul's epiphany

soulxsigh

soul's epiphany

soulxsigh

soul's epiphany

soulxsigh

soul's epiphany

soulxsigh

soul's epiphany

soulxsigh

soul's epiphany

soul's epiphany

Follow me on all social media platforms
@soulxsigh

60575351R00062